My Journey To Freedom

Maura Walsh

authorHOUSE®

AuthorHouse™ UK Ltd.
500 Avebury Boulevard
Central Milton Keynes, MK9 2BE
www.authorhouse.co.uk
Phone: 08001974150

© 2009 Maura Walsh. All rights reserved.

No part of this book may be reproduced, stored in a retrieval system, or transmitted by any means without the written permission of the author.

First published by AuthorHouse 11/18/2009

ISBN: 978-1-4490-2372-0 (e)
ISBN: 978-1-4490-2371-3 (sc)

This book is printed on acid-free paper.

Dedicated To Joshua

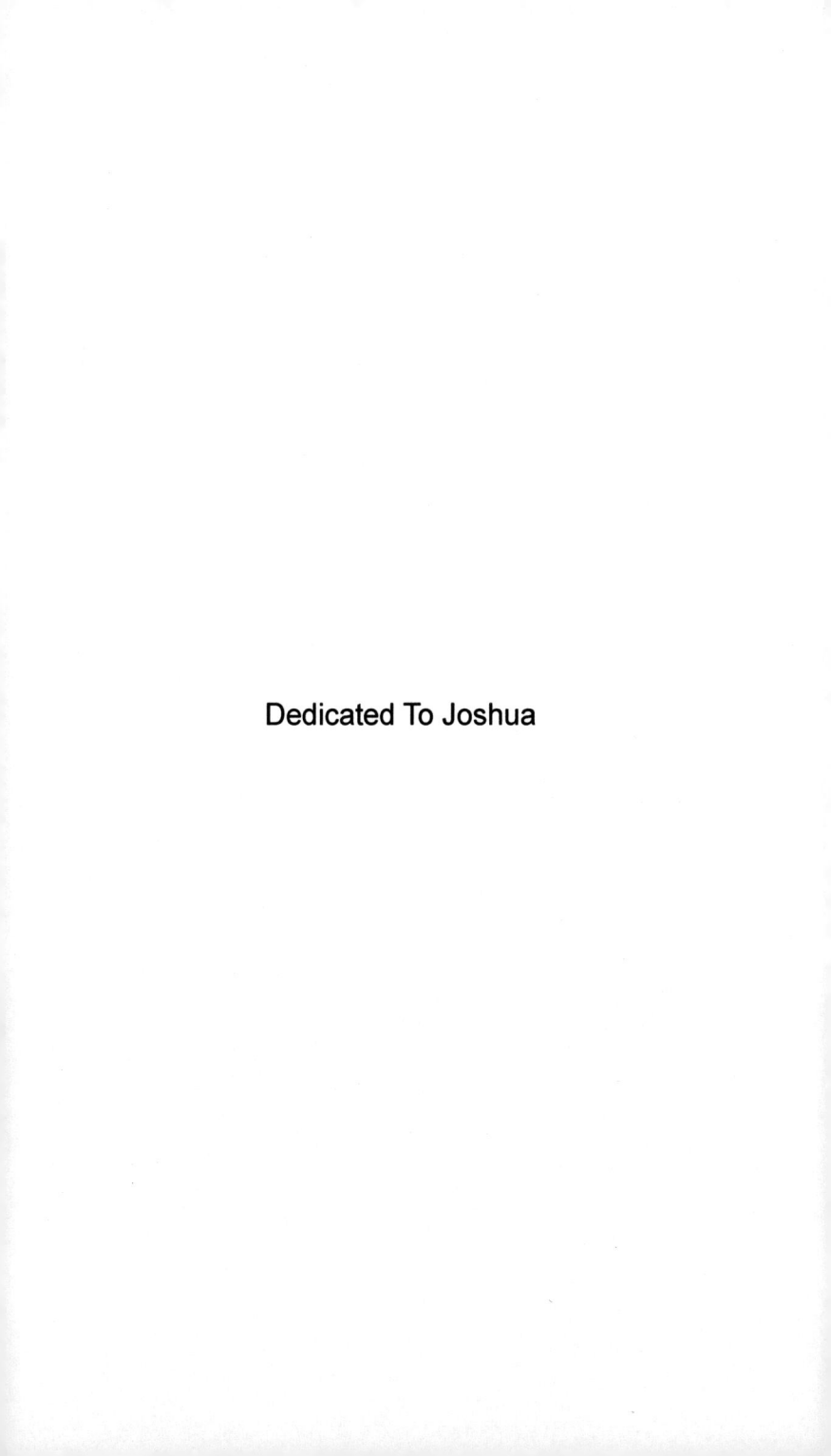

Note

The names of the characters in this book are fictitious to protect their privacy but the story itself is based on fact. It is a sequel to SAM.

INTRODUCTION

Life has many twists and turns along its path, like a road you never know whether it is going to be rough, smooth or what might be just around the next corner.

Let me tell you a story about Jane, feeling frustrated with low self - esteem at her lack of mobility because of her visual impairment. Stuck at a crossroads in her life wondering which way to turn for the best she struggles with decisions to make, wanting to accomplish more in her life but not knowing how to achieve this.

Then along comes a two-year-old Golden Retriever called Sam and her life begins to change for the better. Following their journey together, sometimes difficult, always with humour they travel along learning from all their experiences together gradually building a strong bond until they reach their journey at the present day - firm friends and devoted partners together.

The partnership between owner and a working guide dog is unique, built up with the owner depending on Sam for her life wherever she went and in return Sam becomes a loyal companion and gives her back her freedom and independence that other people take so much for granted.

This story is typical of nearly one thousand new working partnerships formed each year, each story is individual but with a characteristic common to them all of a unique bond between owner and dog no matter whether visual impairment has happened suddenly or gradually.

Chapter 1
A Rough Road

Picture in your mind a woman walking briskly along a country lane, striding confidently with a cream coloured Golden Retriever by her side, listening to birdsong as she walks along. A normal scene in everyday life but it is not, it is exceptional in that the woman is blind and the Golden Retriever is a guide dog. One of many partnerships that are formed each year. The woman is Jane and it is the result of a sequence of events happening over the last few years that she would not have thought possible before. The idea of being able to walk briskly along a country lane again enjoying everything around her, she thought belonged locked in the distant past never to happen again.

I dropped my shopping bags on top of the kitchen work top thankful to be back indoors again, a two hour round trip to go shopping had seemed more like a mad scramble in the January sales leaving me to feel frustrated, tired and wishing not for the first time that a short excursion on a warm spring day could once again be pleasurable instead of an ordeal that was both physically and emotionally tiring.

" Jane stop feeling sorry for yourself and do something about it, this can't go on and you know it " I spoke out loudly trying to vent my feelings on an empty kitchen. Kevin my husband said to me before he went to work that morning to avoid going down our street as they were building new houses and work vans had parked on both pavements as well as a mini digger and further up the road the gas men were digging a hole in the pavement so if I tried to walk past with my cane he would only worry about me. As I needed to go to town I thought I would be sensible and catch a taxi, a good plan but I had forgotten that it was half-term and I was jostled by push chairs, youngsters racing around with shopping trolleys disrupting my train of thought in the shops when I was trying to decide and listen to my memo recorder at the same time what groceries I needed. After the umpteenth time of people bumping into me and one man actually saying "Watch where you are going", I snapped back which was totally out of character for me as I am a tolerant person normally " I'm blind so that might prove to be a little difficult." He mumbled an apology and carried on walking down the aisle. I did have a shopping assistant with me who commented that being half-term, everywhere was busy with children racing around and people

My Journey To Freedom

seemed to be always in a hurry these days with no time to spare.

Crossing roads had its own difficulties. Being careful to cross the road safely I would stand and listen for the traffic. I am sure that the drivers thought that I was either invisible or did not notice that I had got a white cane. Some drivers slowed down sounding the car horn loudly at me so I was then faced with the dilemma of - were they sounding the horn at me thinking that they were being helpful to me in crossing the road? If this was the case, if I had a white cane I obviously had difficulty in seeing the vehicle at all, so how was I able to judge that it was safe enough for me to cross by the driver just sounding the horn, or had they seen someone that they knew on the pavement and were signalling to them. When I explained this to friends and family who could drive they understood my point of view saying that they had not thought about it from a visually impaired person's outlook, they just assumed that they were being helpful. I would still be standing there on the edge of the kerb uncertain what to do but thought it was safer to err on the side of caution. A few drivers did get impatient and shouted at me to hurry up and cross the road but these drivers were in the minority. Crossing at a pedestrian crossing was straightforward as it either made a sound when it was safe to cross or there was a round cylinder that I had been told about, located under the signal box, which vibrated when the lights turned green. A few crossings were not equipped with these methods so these I tried to avoid crossing. Other people who needed to cross as well, thinking that they were also being helpful, would come and stand next to me at the kerb, say "Come along I will get you across", grab my arm and I would be halfway across the road before I knew what had happened not having the time to say no I can manage but thanks for asking. A lot of people would stop at the kerb and ask me if I needed help to cross or was I able to manage. I certainly had to have a sense of humour but the frustration and concern at being safe when I was out and about was always a worry both to myself and my family.

Some people I knew preferred from personal choice to use only a cane and either disliked dogs or didn't want to try any other form of mobility aid. It felt as if I might be making a big mistake jumping out of the frying pan into the fire, I still wasn't sure if I was doing the right thing at all. My brain was getting bombarded with these thoughts and I began to find myself waking up in the night thinking about it. I found it tiring using a cane because it needed all my concentration to get to where I wanted to be. As any visually impaired person will tell you when one sense goes the other senses take over. My hearing became sharper but as this happened gradually over the years I did not realise it was happening. The children as teenagers grumbled they could not get away with things like other teenagers, as I always seemed to know when they tried to creep in later then they

My Journey To Freedom

said they were coming in or I could hear them talking when they thought they could get away with something. A keener sense of smell, learning to recognize people more by their voice and not by the outline of their faces, being more aware of my surroundings by picking up on other people's descriptions to me also listening for clues around me all played a part in my trying to adapt to my changing visual world. As I had lived in my home town for several years, forming visual maps inside my head of my local area was not a problem as I relied on having a good memory, concentrating so hard I was frustrated at my slow pace of walking. This would make me tired so that I lost my train of thought and awareness of exactly where I was causing me to trip over the kerbs. I began to find myself making excuses not to leave the house - it was too windy, raining, the pavements were icy with the frosty weather, any excuse would do. I know I was escaping from the reality of the situation but staying at home or begging friends and family for lifts was easier. Life was difficult and I realised that my world was shrinking as my confidence dropped because of this. I kept on making excuses not to catch the bus into town, to struggle with being jostled in the crowds, having to go around the shops then catching the bus to go back home again all seemed too much to cope with. If I was invited to a strange area or to meet friends in town or a club I either had to have precise instructions how to get there, some people were better at this than others so quite often I got lost if people forgot that road works or street redesigning had taken place, or wait until I could get a lift. Crowded shops were another problem unless I managed to get someone to come with me. I was finding it difficult to find the counter in the shop to get assistance with my shopping unless it was a shop I had known well before my sight deteriorated, provided of course that they hadn't changed the layout of the shop. That would really be confusing and annoying to everybody. I had to be careful to remember not to carry too much shopping as I only had one hand free because of my cane in the other. I could carry shopping in a rucksack but I found sometimes it might overbalance me while I was walking if the pavements were slippery with fallen leaves or icy conditions. It was an ordeal rather than a pleasure to go shopping and getting harder to cope with crowds, mums with push chairs or trolleys that always seemed to be a magnet for me to collide with, busy shopping centres, street furniture and of course trying to shop at Christmas time with even busier conditions than normal became impossible. I had occasional daydreams of what it was like to be able to dash into the shops to buy a few items only taking a few minutes to accomplish, how small actions like this other people in life take for granted instead of the military timing that I had to put into even a small shopping trip when my needs had to fit around other people's schedules. I dismissed these thoughts when I realised that there were other people a lot less fortunate than

My Journey To Freedom

I was when I had family/friends around me for support.

CHAPTER 2

Decisions 2001

So here I was, not really knowing which way to go, decisions to make. Quite often it was one step forward and two steps back when it came to trying to achieve something. My confidence over the years looking back was similar to a roller-coaster ride going up and down depending on what events seemed to be thrown at me at the time.

After being partially sighted since birth I had managed to work for six years in a local factory after bringing up my children Matthew and Caron. After several operations and complications of my original eye condition - Retinopathy of Prematurity, the highs and lows of not knowing how much sight I would eventually be left with resulting in finally being registered blind in 1996. Bringing with it depressive moods, negative thoughts and feelings of frustration at trying to think of coping strategies to deal with family life and what the future held in store for me. Even with all the

My Journey To Freedom

support and help of the family both Matthew and Caron had grown up with Mum's eyes not working as well as they should, frequent tedious waits in hospital outpatient departments and Mum having painful eye operations, only through accepting the situation on a personal level completely could I hope to face what life had to throw at me and to come through the other end a more positive and confident person. This was followed the next year by Rehabilitation College at R.N.I.B. Manor House Torquay for three months and a two-year social care course at R.N.I.B. Loughborough. I enjoyed my time at both colleges mixing with other visually impaired students, exchanging tips and advice about how to manage with a visual problem. I hadn't realised before how many different eye conditions there were affecting all age groups from young students who had been to a blind school to mature students like myself. I was gaining more confidence, realising that besides being a wife and mother I was a person in my own right. Sometimes I felt really motivated to achieve more by a chance remark that another student made or the way other mature students like myself were coping with their difficulties, but I felt something was missing. I was having to study hard and then having to concentrate again on my mobility around college, plus travelling between home and college twice a month as I resided at college during term time. Even with it being familiar to me, it was making me easily tired and the students with guide dogs seemed to find this easier to cope with.

Finding myself still unemployed because of my sight and a heart condition which had been diagnosed since I had been in college, here I was in the spring of 2001 -- my newly found confidence beginning to vanish. I had been thinking over the idea of having a guide dog since meeting students at college with their dogs and noticing how confident they were at moving around college even in unfamiliar areas. Hearing stories from other students how friends had their lives transformed from a shy person having to be led everywhere, no confidence in themselves and in a matter of a few weeks away training with a dog, returning back to college full of confidence. After learning the routes around the college campus, they were able to be totally independent, walking fast and appearing a lot happier about themselves. Suggestions from the children and husband Kevin encouraged the thought to grow and develop into some serious thinking. Kevin, who himself being visually impaired, was finding it difficult to guide me around as well. With the children having flown the nest and now leading independent lives, I could not rely on them so much to take me out or to help me to walk the family dog Flash, so it seemed a good point in my life to make changes. I had not been able to walk him since I returned from college because of my sight problems and as Kevin was at work all day I felt guilty that he

My Journey To Freedom

was not receiving as much exercise and attention as he needed.

When I was at Loughborough College I had met other students who either had guide dogs or were in the process of getting a dog so I was familiar with some aspects of what they did in guiding people around. Some students said it was much better than using a cane even with the extra work that having a dog made and I knew that it took about two years to train a dog. All the problems with my mobility and family concerns finally made up my mind to at least make enquiries about getting a guide dog so I rang up and after explaining my situation they said that they would send someone to make a home visit so we could have a talk about it and see if I was suitable.

A few weeks later Sheila arrived. She was one of the Guide Dog Mobility Instructors. We talked about my situation, whether the garden was large enough so that a dog could spend, my garden not being very big but has a large patio area which Sheila said was ideal, as dogs were trained to spend on both concrete and grass although some dogs could be difficult and would only go on one or the other. She asked me about my lifestyle, saying that if I was suitable to have a guide dog it was very important that she knew what I did as you were not just given a ' dog '. She would have to find a dog to match my personality and my lifestyle and sometimes that is the reason clients have a varied time of waiting as some owners' individual circumstances might mean a longer wait than others. So I explained about my lack of confidence with my mobility problems and general physical fitness, my interests in gardening, going out to blind club meetings, visiting family and friends, wanting to travel more if I had the confidence. It was very important, she said, to match the dog with the potential owner in regard to walking pace, the character of both parties, and the person's lifestyle, which could be very active if the person was young, at work, in college or university or more sedate if the person was elderly and couldn't walk very far. If someone lived in the city travelling by underground and trains each day or lived in a very rural area without any pavements they sometimes required extra training so would I mind going for a walk? I went to get my cane but she said that I wouldn't need it as she had a dog harness. She explained when we were on the pavement that dogs had different speeds of walking and this was a good way to let her know what my general pace of walking was. It must have looked odd to anybody looking as we walked along with Sheila pretending to be the dog. It was only for a few minutes but when we had finished she said that I walked quite quickly and would speed up even faster when my confidence grew. It felt strange when Sheila told me to tell her the commands left and right. I thought to myself " How on earth do I tell a dog to go left, right, forward, straight on", suddenly realising that to have a working dog was entirely different to taking a pet dog for a walk. Sheila assured me that everybody felt like

My Journey To Freedom

this at first but it would soon slot into place. The nearest centre for training was at Leamington Spa in Warwickshire and I would be away from home for about two or three weeks to learn all the commands and training I would need to be able to work with a dog. When the training was finished Sheila said that she would need to come and see me every day for another fortnight to familiarise me with all my normal routes and places that I visited on a regular basis. She said working with a dog was entirely different to using a cane and not to be concerned that after the fortnight we were left alone to struggle. If we had any problems with working, she or another instructor could always be reached by phone with emergency cover at weekends or out of office hours. Any problems or queries could be asked at the annual check-up when she or another instructor would come to the house to see us both. All the vet's bills and the dog food were paid for by Guide Dogs, so anybody on a low income had no need to worry about a high financial expenditure to be paid out each month. She seemed confident that I was suitable to have a dog and that she would be in touch when she had found the right one for me.

So it was about three months later on a warm spring day - a memory that has stayed as sharp as when it happened - unknown to me then, it was going to be the start of my new independent life - that I met a cream, almost white coloured Golden Retriever called Sam. Sheila had telephoned the previous day saying that she thought she had found the right dog for me and would come to see me the next day with Sam to see if we liked each other. I knew that it would have to work both ways. I needed to get on with him and he would have to feel confident with me as well. Feeling very apprehensive ever since the phone call from Sheila sent thoughts racing through my mind. Was I doing the right thing? Would I like him, would he like me, supposing he was not the right dog for me and I was never going to find the right one? Sheila had said on the phone not to worry about it. If Sam was not suitable she felt sure that it would not be difficult to find another dog as sometimes the first choice wasn't right. Was it right having a guide dog or should I manage using a cane and make excuses not to venture far from the house as my confidence had been knocked so many times before, especially with the increase in street furniture and the number of vehicles that we now had on the road?

After an enthusiastic welcome Sheila introduced me to Sam, full of energy and eager for a run around the garden after his car ride. He had been puppy walked locally by Liz Foster who had told Sheila that he had been eager to learn, loved chewing things when he had been younger, a habit which he had grown out of thankfully as he matured. He loved exploring in the garden but was not the type to dig holes. This I was secretly pleased about as gardening was one of my hobbies and I did not want my nicely planted garden borders to turn into muddy holes.

My Journey To Freedom

He could be a little stubborn sometimes but that was a trait of the retriever breed. He was placid, easy-going and always ready for a fuss. Sheila said that she thought we would suit each other but I shouldn't feel obligated, as sometimes it didn't work out when an owner and dog were matched and had started working together. The training would be at Edmondscote Manor, Leamington Spa, the nearest Regional Centre to where I lived, for about two to three weeks. I would learn how to look after Sam, to walk with him avoiding obstacles, in shopping centres, along the street, on and off buses and trains, how to cross the road safely and all traffic conditions as well as all the commands I needed. I told Sheila that it seemed a lot of hard work and as a family we had decided that if I was going to have a guide dog, Flash our family pet dog who was now elderly, was going to be re-homed as we all thought that was for the best with Kevin working all day. Sheila thought that was a good idea as then I could put all my concentration in learning to look after and working with Sam instead of perhaps worrying whether the two dogs would get on well when I returned home. Guide dogs got on with other dogs or other animals if they were with the family but it all depended on family circumstances so each case, Sheila said, was different. She laughed when I said I should find it easy to a certain extent, because I had already had a pet dog, but a working dog was completely different with lots of commands to learn and a strict regime of looking after the dog. As the children had grown up and Kevin did not mind looking after himself for a while, I had no family commitments that would stop me going for training. All the time that we had been chatting together Sam was sitting between the two of us with his head near my knee so I could stroke him. Sheila suggested that we could take him for a short walk just up the street so that I could feel what it was like. She said not to worry about commands, as she would tell me what to say. It certainly felt strange, walking with a dog in this way, but I noticed how carefully Sam moved along with me considering that we were complete strangers to one another. Sheila said that she'd be in touch when there was a place available on the next training course.

Chapter 3

Back To School

Sheila had phoned a few days previously and said could I start at rather short notice because there had been a cancellation due to the summer holidays.

So after saying my goodbyes to the family and promising to be in touch when I had the chance, I was off on what was likely to be one of the biggest decisions that I had made in a long time. Feeling rather apprehensive I arrived at the entrance to the training centre at Edmondscote Manor with a volunteer driver that Guide Dogs use for help with transport. He said never mind the noise, as I would soon get used to it. It was a large Manor House with various extensions that I found out, had been added to over the years. The formal training of guide dogs was first started by Captain Nicolai Liakhoff, a former Officer of the Russian Imperial

Guard who was involved with Guide Dogs until his death in 1962. It was several years later, while I was waiting to catch the bus back home after Sam and I had been out for the day in my nearest town, that I had got chatting to a woman. Having a guide dog always started a conversation going. She was a childhood friend of Captain Liakhoff's family and had known Leamington Spa well and Edmondscote Manor where the family lived. I thought to myself at the time what a small world it was and how complete strangers can be linked together by some distant person or event. The place was alive with dogs barking in the kennel blocks, traffic coming and going and a lot of people around. Apparently some times of the day were busier than others and I just happened to arrive when instructors were going out with clients. After the customary tea/coffee and biscuits with the other potential guide dog owners and being shown around the building we all settled down to start our training. Sheila came and said that I would meet up with Sam again soon as there was plenty to learn in the meantime without him. We were given bags filled with leads, a whistle, grooming equipment, fluorescent Sam Browne belt and armbands for us to use when it was dark or in inclement weather conditions when we were out working with the dogs. Sheila said that during our stay at the Manor we would also have various talks given by instructors on health and safety rules, the law regarding Guide Dogs, grooming,

My Journey To Freedom

first aid, and a general timetable of what we would be doing during our stay each day.

The next morning we were all told to go to our rooms and our instructors would bring our dogs to us. I felt a mixture of feelings, eager to meet Sam again but also anxious, hoping that both Sam and I would be able to cope with the training and qualify together. Sheila had told me that it is also an unsettling time for the dogs, as they have to learn to transfer their loyalty from the instructor they had been with for several months working together to another completely different person, who would behave in an unsure manner with them to begin with. It confused them as well because in only two years they probably had at least two or three different homes, leaving their mothers to go to puppy-walkers, then on to advanced training with perhaps one or two instructors and finally dog owners like I hoped to be. Sam was pleased to see me when Sheila brought him into the room. The feeling was mutual and he came to put his head on my knee for a fuss. Sheila explained that now Sam would stay with me for the rest of the training, sleeping in a basket that was provided in the bedroom. Sam of course had done all his advanced training with Sheila and now had to not only remember everything that he had learnt, but transfer his loyalty to me so that we could qualify together and hopefully become a working team. "Now training really has begun" she said with a laugh as we all went downstairs to learn about grooming, involving cleaning their teeth daily and checking their paws for any injury while they had been working especially important in the winter with icy pavements that might have grit or salt on them. It caused a laugh as everybody else had yellow or black Labradors with short-haired coats so they always finished grooming long before I did. Sam of course was cream with his long fluffy retriever coat that caused me to spend longer session times in grooming. It was then that I discovered as well that Retrievers moult a lot!

The next few days flew by in a blur of learning the correct position of walking with Sam, walking commands of forward, straight on, hup-up to speed up, steady to slow down, right, left and back given from a standstill to indicate a complete change of direction, over to ease the dog over to the left, in to move to the right. As well as some hand and foot signals to use we worked on basic obedience commands of sit, down, stay, wait, leave when Sheila was not with us to keep Sam concentrating and alert. We had started to do basic traffic work of walking down the street, Sam, sitting at kerbs while I listened for traffic then telling him to go forward to cross the road. Sheila of course was always with us - reminding me sometimes when I forgot a command - the first time that Sam refused a command to go forward when I thought the road was clear but then a bicycle came whizzing quickly by. I had not heard it all and I felt a sudden surge of dismay that Sam had not obeyed me. Then, as Sheila was telling me that it would take quite a time before I trusted him completely, I remembered that

My Journey To Freedom

she had told me that I must learn not to doubt him. It was all new and I wasn't sure whether I was going to remember everything as it was a long time since I had been to school! Sheila said that everybody felt the same way having a few doubts and not feeling very confident in the beginning as it was so different to just walking a pet dog if you were sighted. It did seem entirely different to just walking with a pet dog and giving simple commands. It was the thought that everything depended on how we bonded together and that I would have to completely put all my trust and depend on my new companion for my life.

It was not all work and no play as we all fortunately got on together as a group and were able to chat about our experiences as we were training and we had good social evenings in which we were able to unwind at the end of our day talking together or asking any member of staff about any concerns we had.

There were large free run areas fenced in at the back of the kennels where we could take the dogs two at a time to run off any surplus energy they might have, to have fun time with the other dogs and to get the dogs to go and play on command, come back to us combining a command with a whistle and the use of one or two pellets of food as a treat with plenty of praise. Chew bones or a few pellets of food were used as part of the training and afterwards as a reward when they worked hard. The dogs were all fed on strict guidelines with the food weighed at each meal, they had to sit and wait until a whistle was blown and told that they could start eating. This strictness was necessary because if they did become overweight as working dogs it might interfere with them being able to guide properly so it would be a mistake if they were allowed to be overfed or to be given a lot of scraps. Also as Sheila said, if they got used to being fed scraps when they went to a restaurant, or to other people's houses and food was about, they could easily begin to scrounge for food and it would give Guide Dogs a bad reputation. Labradors especially, are notorious scavengers and take every opportunity to get to food whenever they can. Sheila told some of us a story of a Labrador that managed to open the kitchen cupboard where its food was kept and ate a large quantity and had to be rushed to the vets for treatment! Of course events happen occasionally when a guide dog might be tempted by taking food or a child/ member of the public might give the dog food without the owner being aware of the situation resulting in the dog perhaps having an upset stomach and then the owner would be wondering why. The dogs had all been taught that before going for a walk and then on returning they had to go and " spend". This was always called busy-busy, so that they would not have any accidents while they were out working, so even a short walk in the future with Sam was going to mean planning beforehand what I had to remember to do. With everything to learn, grooming, being shown how to put the

My Journey To Freedom

harness on, avoiding obstacles, beginning on harness work on the street and giving Sam free time to play the days were filled with plenty to do and think about. I enjoyed our evenings together as we gathered with other students to talk about our day's adventures or we just had a quiet time in the bedroom when Sam was off harness and loved me to make a fuss of him. It was all part of the bonding process. I spoke to the family most nights depending on their work commitments telling them what we had both been up to during the day. They all said that they were missing me and looking forward to having us at home.

Chapter 4
Qualifying

We carried on training each day, combining more into our schedule that we had learnt. Several of us were taken into the town centre each day to walk on different routes in and around the shopping centre. The first couple of times seemed strange with Sheila, as I had been so used to finding my way with a cane. Now I had Sam to be my guide, weaving in and out of the crowds avoiding everybody instead of using my cane and frequently bumping into people or catching my ankle on people's push chairs. When we had done the route a few times I began to get used to this different mode of mobility and started to look forward to our town centre training. There were plenty of shops to go to. Sheila taught me how to go into lifts, walking up and down different stairs which included open tread stairs, as some dogs were put off by being able to see the ground as they walked up or down. To find out where the

My Journey To Freedom

shop doorways were, to find the counter of the shop and how to find if there was a queue, by giving Sam instructions and explaining the layout of where the shops were. She said it would be easier when I went home, as I already knew the layout of the shops that I regularly used. I told Sheila how pleased it made me and how easy it seemed, compared to having to have someone with me to find the counter as I had had to do before, to be able to tell Sam to find the counter in the shop so that I could get assistance with my shopping and he went straight away to where he needed to be. I know to a sighted person it would be a very small accomplishment when they go shopping, something which they would do automatically without thinking, but to me I felt really independent especially when I did it the first couple of times. Sheila laughed saying that was what Sam was for, to give me my independence back and to make life easier for me. A couple of times we went into the cafe in the shopping centre so that Sheila could show me the correct way to order a snack with Sam sitting patiently in the queue, tell Sam to find a seat and then remove his harness while we had a well earned rest with a cup of tea and Sam curled up as much as he could under the table out of harm's way.

We had already done some obstacle work in the grounds of the Manor with various items put in our path that Sam had to guide me around, people would suddenly block our way or Sam would have to weave around several items in a line. Sheila began also to show us how to avoid different obstacles on the pavement as we were walking along which included obstacles above me and how to go around cafe furniture outside pubs, bicycles that had been flung down in shop doorways, street cleaners with trolleys, people in wheelchairs, crowds of teenagers gathering outside shops. Sam seemed to delight in picking up his pace and going straight, weaving in and out of the crowds. At times it gave me the feeling of the parting of the waves as people seemed to move out of Sam's way. By Sheila telling me were she wanted Sam to go, by his walking pace slowing and how his movement felt through his harness I could tell what he was doing. When something blocked the pavement completely like a wheelie bin Sheila taught me how to do an " off kerb " which means that Sam stopped and sat down, telling me his path was blocked, I told him to find the kerb and I listened for traffic to make sure it was safe then told him to off kerb. He then went out into the road going around the obstacle and then back onto the pavement. Sometimes instead I told him to find another way if I thought that our path was blocked or if we were walking down the street and we came across road works or scaffolding around a building and that part of the pavement was closed, we'd retrace our steps to find a safer route.

Sheila showed me how to remove Sam's harness when getting on buses and trains so that

My Journey To Freedom

he could curl himself under the seat to keep out of other people's way. We went to the train station in the minibus with other students and dogs of course so it was a bit of a tight squeeze, to get the experience of people rushing up and down the long stairways and to get used to the noise of the station with Sam guiding me. When we left the station walking back to the minibus Sheila told me to tell Sam to " find the car ". I obeyed but was very doubtful, as the car park was large and must have had a lot of vehicles in it. There was no need to doubt Sam's ability, he seemed to quicken his pace and start looking around. I could feel this by the movement of the harness, as he headed straight to a place stopped and sat down and waited. I asked Sheila, who was following behind with some of the other students, was Sam right and she said " Yes exactly right by the side of the minibus." How he did it I'm not sure, whether he picked up the scent of were he had been but I gave Sam lots of praise and told him how clever he was. Apparently he had just started to do it one day when Sheila by chance told him to find the vehicle that they had come in. Thinking about it afterwards I found just walking with Sam amongst a crowd of people, feeling at ease for the first time, made me much more aware of what was going on around me and contrasted to how I would have been before, perhaps being guided by someone else with my cane feeling anxious at being jostled by the crowds and trying to manage the long stairways with everybody rushing past me.

Towards the end of our course we concentrated on advanced traffic work. Sheila and other instructors would set up a scene usually managing to find a quiet side street that they used frequently for this purpose. I would tell Sam to go forward to cross the street when an instructor would deliberately drive towards us without warning, making sure that Sam disobeyed me and did not panic. I would also tell Sam to cross the road at a certain point that Sheila told me about, knowing that it was not safe there because of parked cars in our way. Sam was expected to disobey me and find a safer crossing point. I was rather uneasy about doing this part of the course but I knew that we were in a controlled situation and it was good experience in case of unexpected traffic conditions when we went home. We all talked about it that evening and the students like myself who had never had a guide dog before, had all felt the same way which made me feel a lot better. The students who were on their second, third, or fourth dogs all took it in their stride as part of the course. A couple of days before our due date for leaving the course Sheila came up to me and told me to meet her that evening with several others in the hallway after tea when it was dark. I asked why and she said it was for a night walk to see what we were like working in the dark as Sam might react differently to shadows, street lights, strange noises and not to worry it was all

My Journey To Freedom

part of the course and only meant a short walk out of the Manor grounds, down the street and round in a circle back up the steps to the Manor. She must have seen my look of uncertainty and smiled saying that instructors would be around somewhere but I wouldn't know where. I felt that it was one thing beginning to trust Sam in the daylight in town and crossing roads, but it was an entirely different matter in the dark. I went cautiously with Sam as he took me carefully down the Manor steps into the street, hoping that Sam worked well and everything would be all right. My doubts proved to be groundless I need not have worried at all. Sam walked normally without a hint of hesitating at shadows or anything in his way. I walked confidently back up the manor steps again praising Sam telling him that he had been a good boy for me, feeling relief that it had gone well. Sheila met me saying " I was watching you both working well together, I knew that you'd both be ok." " It's Sam who worked hard. I just followed" I said laughing, as we headed back inside for a well earned rest.

Various instructors gave us short talks about how to clean the leather harness with saddle soap to keep it in good condition, Health and Safety Regulations concerning Guide Dogs in shops and restaurants, as they were by law allowed anywhere but it could be a problem when guide dog owners were refused permission by people who did not understand about the law, visits to the vets, not to use escalators in case the dogs caught their paws in the moving steps. This included not carrying them on the escalators as well because of safety reasons and the dogs were too heavy. This conjured up a funny image in my mind of someone struggling with a large German Shepherd or Retriever so I couldn't help but laugh aloud. I think everybody in the room had simultaneously had the same image because we all laughed at this. We were told about the dangers of fireworks, being careful if we needed to work with them on a hot day. If we needed to use taxis it was always a good idea to let them know that you had a guide dog with you and then taxi firms could sometimes send a larger cab for you or change drivers if one of them were allergic to dog hair. There certainly was a lot to think about.

We were all wondering in anticipation if we had passed the course. It was the day before we were to go home. Sam and I had just completed another route going into town and were waiting for the bus when Sheila came up beside several of us saying " Well done you've all passed. We've arranged to go out for a meal tonight to celebrate." We all arrived back at the centre in a flurry of excitement congratulating one another and giving our dogs a big fuss. Sheila took Sam and I into the office to sign our paperwork, collect our Guide Dog badges and ID wallets that contained details of vets, puppy walkers, ownership details and for me to pay the princely sum of fifty pence! This was for the transfer of ownership of Sam to me but guide dogs would still maintain control and

My Journey To Freedom

reserve the right if they, at any time, thought that the dogs were being ill treated or not worked properly they could take them away from the owner. They also help in finding homes if the dogs are not remaining with their owners when they reach retirement age at about nine or ten years of age. The instructor would come and see us both annually and routine six monthly visits to the vets with a health report that had to be sent back to guide dogs each time, were compulsory. When the charity first started it was agreed that a small sum of money should be exchanged because they were a charity so that an owner, regardless of their financial situation, could have a dog and the sum has remained the same for a number of years now. I was also surprised to learn that guide dogs are one of the leading supporters of ophthalmic research into blindness, that they rely entirely on public donations, legacies and fundraising and do not receive any government funding. The next day was spent in getting ourselves and dogs, equipment and luggage packed and ready for our return home. We also had a class photograph taken of everybody with their dogs, every one of them sitting perfectly still. I was looking forward to returning home as I had missed Kevin and the children even though I phoned them nearly every night telling them everything that Sam and I had been up to. I felt that it was going to be a new start for me with Sam even with not having properly bonded with him yet and facing a lot of challenges as we learned to live and work together.

Chapter 5

A Door Opens

Sheila drove us home with the back of the car loaded up with Sam, my luggage, dog bowls, food and dog equipment. Kevin met us at the front door to welcome us back home and Sam was excited to get out of the car and stretch his legs. We went into the house and let Sam into the garden so that he could have his first sniff exploring around his new home. Sheila said that she would see us again the next day when we would begin the next part of our training to learn how to work with Sam around all my usual regular routes in my home area as well as local train stations and places that I visited frequently, so after a quick cup of tea we were left to spend our first family night together. Kevin and I gave Sam lots of fuss and as Sam had been used to sleeping in my bedroom at the centre we put his dog mat at the foot of our bed and his dog basket in the sitting room so he could please himself where he slept. I was tired after

My Journey To Freedom

our journey so after making sure Sam had been outside to busy-busy and he seemed comfortable I went up the stairs to bed. A couple of minutes later I could hear the patter of feet and Sam came into the bedroom settling down on his mat as if he had been doing this routine for ages instead of his first night in a strange house. I smiled to myself thinking that already Sam was making himself at home. I had arranged for Matthew and Caron to call round the next evening after they had both finished work to meet Sam and to hear all about my adventures at school!

The next morning I was up bright and early as I wasn't sure exactly what time Sheila was coming as she had a few visits to make before she came to see us. I had breakfast, put Sam out for an early morning run round the garden and fed him at 8.00 a.m. I had found out at the centre he was punctual about what time he had his meals and seemed to have a built in clock! His teeth were cleaned, coat brushed and harness ready to be put on as soon as Sheila arrived. Sheila came shortly afterwards and after giving Sam a fuss who welcomed her warmly, I put Sam out for busy-busy before we got started, then put his harness on and we were off. Sheila said it was best to start off with a short walk around the block which incorporated our nearest post-box, one of the bus stops I used to get into Kettering and my nearest corner shop. I felt strange as I knew it was going to be easier than using my cane. I had found this out at the training centre and I was familiar with my local area and as I said before, had built up a mental picture of where I was but I still had to get rid of all my feelings of insecurity when I used my cane and really try to start to trust and bond with Sam. It felt strange telling Sam were I needed to go after Sheila told me which direction she wanted us to go in. Straight on, left, right, first small side street crossed and then the main road. Sam headed straight for the post-box as directed. We crossed the road safely even though I felt unsure at what I was doing. I knew what to do but it was a case of putting everything together that I had learnt, of trusting Sam, learning to work with him and trusting in my own abilities as well as Sam's. I paused and praised Sam after touching the post-box just to make sure we had made it, walked down the street to the bus stop, found the safest place to cross as we had to go round a corner and indent to find a straight part of the pavement again onto the corner shop where Sam was greeted with people wanting to know when I had got back from training, what my dog's name was, how old he was and could they stroke him so I stopped, put Sam's harness handle down which indicated to Sam that we had stopped working and paused for a chat with them and Sheila for five minutes. I listened to my watch and was really surprised that I had done the walk in far less time than it usually took me with my cane and realised that besides having at the moment to concentrate harder on following what Sheila was saying, telling Sam where I needed to go and

My Journey To Freedom

trusting in Sam to guide me safely all at the same time I did not feel tense and uptight like I normally would. We headed back home for a well earned cup of tea and a chew bone for Sam. I phoned Kevin straight away to tell him how we had got on with our first walk as he was at work. Sheila said that we had done well as it was strange for the both of us the first time but would get easier as we did more routes together. It was quite a family gathering that evening when Matthew and Caron came round and played with Sam in the garden giving him loads of fuss which Sam loved as retrievers like a lot of attention.

The next few days were spent in Sheila coming round each day and we went to the doctor's, dentist's, chemist's, library and a visit to the vet's in the nearest town where I lived to introduce Sam and to book his first six monthly check up. I was surprised to find out that Sam was already known by John the vet as Liz Foster who puppy walked Sam used to take him to another branch of the same veterinary practice so John on occasions had seen Sam before. They met each other like old friends and not at all like most dogs seeing the vet. My own experience with our dog Flash was virtually dragging him along the waiting room floor towards the surgery door and then a continuing battle to get him into the surgery for treatment. It's something to do with the smell they pick up from other anxious animals I was told. Also guide dogs both as puppies and adults, visit the vet's more than a pet dog would as part of their social interaction with people and other animals.

A small enclosed park was only three streets away. We went to see it with Sheila one morning so she could tell me if it was safe to let Sam off the lead for a free run. I took some of Sam's food pellets with me for a treat and after Sheila had a good look round I told Sam he deserved a run around. I took off his harness and lead and put his ordinary collar on with a small bell attached so that when it jingled I could judge whereabouts he was. I gave him two small pellets as an incentive to come back as Sheila said it was a good idea as we had never been there before and Sam went off for a good smell and sniff round. Sheila said Sam kept coming back towards me to check on where I was she said he was exactly the same at the centre and only really had a proper play when other dogs were around for a playful chase together. I blew my whistle to recall Sam and he came bounding along quite happily straight away nudging my hand to tell me that he had come back wanting the small pellets of food I had ready for him for a treat as he came back straight away. Sheila said we'd better hurry up and walk back home as it was just starting to spit with rain and judging from the colour of the clouds any minute it might pour down before we had a chance to get back home. We did not make it and trudged along with rain dripping down our waterproofs which thankfully we put on that morning, walking in a straight line along the pavement I felt Sam veer slightly to one

My Journey To Freedom

side and then carried on. He did this three times and each time I found out that I had to go through the puddles. I didn't stop but told Sheila when we arrived back what I thought Sam had done and why had he done it as Sheila had been following us and could see how Sam worked. She burst out laughing and said " It hasn't taken him long to settle down in some ways. He was exactly the same at the centre if it was raining and Liz told me he was the same as a puppy. He might be a retriever but he hates getting his feet wet in puddles so he makes sure that whoever he is with has to go through the puddles instead. They are all trained as guide dogs in the same way but each one has its own little characteristics that come out so you'll have to learn what Sam's are and react accordingly."

It seemed strange on my first visits to the doctor's, the library and the chemist that were all in the same small area. As Sheila said it was a good idea to get my bearings that way as working with a dog was different to what I had been used to. I arrived at the doctor's surgery door after telling Sam to find left and then find the door. I had to touch the door to make sure that Sam had led me to the right place! I was still doubtful but getting better. it really was strange at first to give " a dog " commands of where I needed to go resulting in being guided to exactly the right place. Sheila made the comment when we had five minutes break by the door that this is why it takes a good six months or even longer to really bond with the dog as you have to really trust the dog to take you to where you want to go. After our first few local trips Sheila said that as it was the weekend we had done well and she would see me again on Monday morning. It wouldn't do any harm to attempt a few of our short routes by myself with Sam and to let her know after the weekend how we had both got on. Then we could catch the bus into town to tackle some of the more difficult routes.

After telling Sam to sit and wait while I unlocked the front door I felt proud of myself with a real feeling of being independent without the usual tense or anxious feelings that I had been used to. It does not sound a big achievement but to me it felt like a real milestone that I had accomplished telling Kevin we were both safely back after our first walk together without getting lost.

I had got ready to go and told Kevin this was it and we were going to the post box and the corner shop to let him know which direction we were heading in just in case I got into difficulties on the way and off we went. We had been to the post box after crossing the road which I did without feeling so unsure in what I was doing trying to remember everything that Sheila had said to me about road crossings, onto the corner shop for some milk including of course a chat with people on our way wanting to know about Sam and how I was getting on, retracing our steps back home again. Kevin said he was really pleased with me, well us both really and we'd have a lot to tell Sheila on Monday. It wasn't until a few weeks later when he said that he had something to tell me with a chuckle that as soon as I had gone out of the front door that first time he had gone out of the back door and followed me on my journey until I had nearly reached home to make sure that I was all right. He then quickly got back inside the house and sat down watching television pretending that he had been there all the time!!

On Monday after checking the bus timetable we waited at the bus stop for the bus to take us into Kettering so that Sam and I could familiarize ourselves with the easiest route to take to do our shopping and to visit the bank. I didn't use the " hole in the wall " and I never had because as a visually impaired person I felt rather vulnerable standing in a queue trying to use the cash point and if I took longer than normal I wouldn't know if anybody might be looking over my shoulder at my pin number, so I preferred to take my money out as cash back when I went shopping or at the bank counter. It felt different on the bus as the bus driver recognised me and held everybody up while he asked me the name of my dog and how I was getting on. As Sheila said I would have to get used to this, as when you had a guide dog everybody either wanted to stop you for a chat and make a fuss of the dog or walked by in complete silence thinking that they did not want to interrupt our concentration. We worked out that for me depending on where, of course I wanted to do my shopping in the future, that to get off at the library was the best for me. Then I could negotiate my way past the church, the market, cross the crossing, past a few shops and on my right find the bank which was the only building along there with an automatic opening door that I could recognise by the sound it made. We entered the bank and I told Sam to find the counter of course the staff made a fuss of him. Afterwards we went to a couple of shops that we needed to go to and then found our way around the indoor shopping centre where I told Sheila which shops I used on a regular basis. I was beginning to get tired with all the concentration so Sheila suggested that we finished and we retraced our steps back to the bus stop. Suddenly I found Sam trying to turn left near the automatic door of the bank and Sheila quickly told me to tell him in a firm voice to go straight on which he did. She explained as we were waiting for the bus that Sam was like that sometimes and thought ahead of what he thought that I wanted to do and he had anticipated that because we had gone into the bank as we went up the street we would logically want to go there again when we came back down the street. Sheila said working with Sam was going to be interesting and I wouldn't find it so tiring as we started to get used to each other more but I would have to learn to speak firmly to Sam quickly when the need arose like the anticipation at the bank door or it might lead to problems later on with him going to places that he wanted to go to and I didn't.

My Journey To Freedom

For the next few days we were kept busy by Sheila. We visited a smaller market town called Market Harborough lying in the opposite direction to Kettering that I sometimes visited when a member of the family could take me. I knew the layout of the main buildings, shops and the streets in the town fairly well as I once lived there so could still visualise them. Sheila took me in the car this time for a change parking in the nearest car park so it was an easy walk to the pedestrian walkway leading to the shops and a large indoor market that was open three times a week. When we had finished I told Sam as we approached the car park again to find the car. He started immediately to quicken his pace. Sheila said " He's heading straight towards the car. We'd never get lost with Sam around." which made us both laugh. It was also within walking distance from the market bus stop to the vet's that I went to with Sam and as Sheila said it was handy to know exactly where the nearest bus stops were situated in relation to the vet's in case I needed them in the future if no one could bring me by car. She also said that if I was feeling adventurous there was a large park with a purpose built dog run that was completely safe to use on the outskirts of the town that I could take Sam to. We had several visits into Kettering including the train station to get Sam used to it as Sheila said that if I was planning a train journey she could help if I had any problems but if I let train staff know in advance of any journey I could book tickets as well as getting help on and off the train and in and out of the station itself. I needed to know where certain shops were including the post office and the large supermarket we normally used. I found out that the shop had two entrances, one we always used and another that had revolving doors. That must have been the reason that no one had told me about it as just using my cane and trying to negotiate the revolving doors I think would have proved difficult to say the least. Sheila said she wasn't sure if Sam had used revolving doors before but it was a good idea to try them while she was with us in case of problems. Sam sat down and waited patiently while I listened for the doors to come around and I told him to go forward. I could feel him through the harness hesitating as he must have been weighing up the situation walking forward through the doors and out the other side without any problems at all. I stopped and praised him Sheila saying that we had both dealt with that well as I had trusted Sam to work it out for himself which he had done and we thankfully went on to find the customer service desk in the shop to introduce Sam and to pick up a few items that I needed while I was there. Despite everything still being fairly new Sheila said she thought we were both doing well with our mobility and it looked as if we had been together for longer than we had. This comment made me feel that I was really progressing with Sam she said she would probably only be coming out to see us once more. I was not to rush things but to familiarize myself doing the routes alone that we had done,

My Journey To Freedom

gradually doing more each day. Sam only had to do a route once and he remembered where to go which I thought was remarkable. I was not to worry as she said I had no long distance routes that I needed help with in the near future but just to phone up if I had any problems or queries with Sam, to fill in my report each day. I worked Sam so that when she came for her next visit we could iron out any problems that I had noticed if any. She had also mentioned that it was a good idea to keep up with giving Sam obedience lessons on a regular basis as it kept him alert.

Chapter 6

Independence

During Sheila's last visit I had arranged to see the vet for Sam's first check-up and then we were going to do any routes I needed to go on before I saw Sheila on her next visit to us. Sam was excited as he always was when I started to get ready to go out. He followed me everywhere in the house. Sheila said it was part of the bonding process always wanting to know where I was. He'd wait outside the bathroom door until I came out again and would sit on his mat in the bedroom while I changed to go out not wanting to miss anything. We caught the bus to the vets with Sam curled up as much as he could under the seat while Sheila and I talked. There was a bus stop near the vets that Sheila had showed me on the day we went into the town for a look round so I knew both the bus stop from the direction of getting off from home to the vet and the one at the market bus stop where I could then walk to the vet's if

My Journey To Freedom

needed. The vet wasn't John that we saw and after he examined Sam saying that he was fine, filling in the health book that was required with each visit and a copy that I had to send to Guide Dogs. After we came out of the vet's Sheila said that Sam looked quite dejected when he realised that it wasn't John he was going to see, " Trust me to have a dog who loves going to see the vet " I replied. Sheila told me that it was quite common when the dogs settled into their new homes that some of them would put on extra weight because perhaps they took slightly less exercise than when they were at the centre and they were content to be in one place and not having to change owners as they were before. I should remember to have him weighed at each visit.

It was a Thursday and a few days after Sheila's last visit. I intended to do a walk each day and today was market day in the town. I told Sam to find the kerb and he sat down obediently as we had to cross the main road by the post box to walk down to the market, " Forward Sam " Sam did not move at all but I could not hear any noise so I told him again " Come on Sam forward ". I began to get a little impatient with a rising sense of panic thinking that I was giving him the wrong command or Sam was being difficult. Suddenly a voice said " Hello Jane, how are you and Sam getting on? " It was an acquaintance that a friend had introduced me to previously. I said " Oh hello, Sam doesn't want to cross over the road, can you see anything in his way? I can't hear anything wrong ". He replied "The reason Sam isn't doing as you told him is that they have mended that stretch of road on the opposite side next to the kerb that the Water Board got up. You must have been away when they did it and they have left cones around it for a few days because there is still a small hole until they have completely finished it. If I was you for the next few days I would cross further down the road." Gratefully I said "Thanks for telling me I was beginning to think that he was being difficult ". Alan gave Sam an affectionate pat on the head saying " Glad to help, see you again ". I told Sam to come on and to go straight on so that we could cross further down the road as Alan had suggested, telling Sam how good I thought that he had been and hoping that as time went on I could trust Sam completely. My panic had instantly vanished as soon as I knew what had happened and instead I felt relieved that I had got Sam to look after me and I suddenly had a vision of what might have happened if I had been using my cane, crossed the road there which was my usual place and walked straight into the cones. I might have injured myself badly and even if I had only escaped with bruising I think it would have also knocked my confidence badly stopping me from going out. I shuddered at the thought and said to Sam that I'd buy him a treat at the pet stall in the market. The market was not very big only about six stalls but I liked to get my fresh vegetables and fruit at one of the stalls as they were a great deal cheaper than the supermarket, as long as I

My Journey To Freedom

didn't get carried away and have to carry heavy shopping bags back home again. I introduced Sam to the man who had the pet stall as I often got seed for the bird table from him. He made a fuss of Sam who sat quite still sniffing the air which I'm sure was filled with delicious smells of various pet treats. I told Kevin about our adventure that evening when he returned from work and he said that he would have told me about the road works but he had not been down that side of the road for a while to notice it and what a good thing it was that I'd got Sam with me at the time. I put it in my report that I had to fill in for Sheila so that I wouldn't forget to mention it the next time that I saw her.

For the next few weeks I took Sam out on short routes into town trying to go somewhere different each day to build up routines for us so that I gained more confidence with him before we went into Kettering on the bus to do some shopping, even if it was only going to the shop or the post box. The weather was still mild with sunny days and when we went to the local shops I noticed that one of Sam's favourite stops was the butcher's because it had a cool floor he could lie on while I was waiting to be served! My journeys to and from the shops took much longer now as friends and people that we didn't know would ask me if it was all right to stop me in the street to make a fuss of Sam. I always replied that as long as Sam and I were not working meaning that Sam had stopped and I was no longer holding onto the handle of his harness and we had stopped at a bus stop or waiting in a queue quietly, I did not mind if people came up to us to ask about Sam or wanting to stroke him. There was a warning on the handle part of the harness saying PLEASE DON'T DISTRACT ME I'M WORKING. The majority of people took notice of this with a few asking what was written on the harness before they had chance to read it but there were always a few who tried to stroke Sam as we were walking down the street. With these I had to be firm, explaining why it was necessary to insist that Sam wasn't distracted while he was working. When I did explain that it could be dangerous to me if Sam's attention was allowed to wander - bumping into lamp posts, falling over street furniture outside shops, workmen mending holes on the pavement - the list goes on. If it was a child and I explained to the parent they were very understanding. Very often as Sam and I were walking down the street we would overhear when children were passing, " Look that's the lady with a special dog. It's working and we mustn't stroke it " or a young child would ask the adult with them why that thing (harness) was on the dog and I often heard the adult patiently replying that it was called a working dog and it was helping to guide me because I could not see. I began to feel proud and really felt that Sam and I were becoming partners. Sometimes Kevin came with me on our walks but he always walked behind me as he said if he walked beside me the pavements were not wide enough and if he was in front of me it might encourage Sam to just follow him and not work independently.

I think at this time that Sam and I were settling down slowly together, he would follow me everywhere in the house and when I went to get his harness from behind the front door he sat eagerly waiting for me to put it on so we could go out. When he went busy-busy he seemed to know that it signalled another walk and perhaps somewhere different to go. I was gradually getting more accustomed to my freedom at being able to go out on my own, just being able to say to whoever was in the house at the time, " See you later I'm going to .... ", surprised me at first in how saying a few words could change my whole outlook on life and give me a more positive attitude in myself that had always been there but had become buried because of my feelings of frustration and how I had felt before. Instead of getting frustrated at missed appointments or waiting for other people to find the time to take me to where I needed to be. Sam's easy going character meant that he didn't seem to be bothered by anything on the walks so far that we had done but Sheila had warned me that he was a Golden Retriever and that they could sometimes be very stubborn or difficult when they were working wanting to do their own thing. Sam was keen to go into the butcher's because of the cool floor and smells and would always take me to the door even if I had no shopping to do in the butchers. He also tended to anticipate what he thought I wanted to do like taking me to the dentist's for an appointment one day and then because we happened to pass the surgery the next day he stopped at the door thinking that I wanted to go back again, not my favourite place to visit once let alone the next day as well ! Sam liked to keep to his own routines whenever I went to the hairdresser's. He got into the habit of going towards the same chair that we used. If the chair was occupied or they were busy and we had to use another chair he apparently looked most put out. I remembered what Sheila had said about retriever stubborn moments and laughed to myself. She said that as long as I was able to anticipate these stubborn times and could be strict when they happened it should be all right. I had gone out at night a couple of times and on one side of the pavement there were high hedges that overhung the path that rustled in the wind. Sam carried on regardless of any strange noises. Sheila had told me that sometimes strange noises like fireworks going off suddenly or shadows at night can startle the dogs so much that they become too nervous to work and have to be retired so I would have to be careful around November time and try and keep Sam indoors in the evening when I heard fireworks being let off. Sam's attitude to wet weather soon became a family joke. One week we had to put up with two days of almost constant rain so I felt reluctant to take Sam very far as I didn't fancy getting soaking wet. First of all Sam waited at the back door to be let out after breakfast for busy-busy which he always did I opened the

My Journey To Freedom

door and he sat there apparently looking up at me Kevin said as if by some magical powers I was able to turn off the rain long enough for him to go out! I had to really encourage and coax him to go outside. In the end he dashed outside rushing to go under some shrubs, did what he had to do and dashed back inside again as quickly as he could. He worked well in the rain the same as he always did but he seemed to have an air of I will work properly but I don't like to in the wet and walk with a heavier tread. When it came to puddles he would veer slightly to one side narrowly avoiding the puddle just enough to keep his paws dry and I would always get wet shoes! If the puddle was large he would stop and if it was not covering the whole of the pavement he could find a way around it otherwise he did an off kerb move into the road and back onto the pavement again.

It was at this time that I remembered that I had told Sheila that I would get in touch with Liz Foster, Sam's puppy walker. So one day after I had filled in that day's report that nothing had happened and Sam had worked well I phoned her up and told her that we were settling down together and I would send a photo when Matthew came to see us bringing his camera with him. Liz told me that it was lovely to hear from me as not all the qualified owners had kept in touch with her regarding news of the puppies that she had puppy walked. She told me that it was true that Sam had disliked puddles ever since she had him as a small puppy which caused us both to have a good laugh. Besides that he learned everything quickly and was always eager to find out what was going on and to do new things which sometimes had led him into scrapes, chewing things and being accident prone by sniffing things in the garden like nettles or a hedgehog! When he was a small puppy he went out into the snow and Liz had to rescue him as he had jumped out of the back door and sunk up to his chest and couldn't move. He sounded quite a scamp when he was younger. Sam also had a brother called Sandy who successfully qualified at the same time and she had not heard from Sandy's new owner yet.

Chapter 7

Teamwork

Life now took on a whole new meaning for me. Instead of staying at home making excuses not to go out I was eager to become more independent. I think that Kevin was becoming less concerned now that he no longer had the worry about my mobility and would encourage me to go out every day with Sam to build up our confidence. The family, Matthew and Caron and my friends were pleased to see a change in me, listening to my tales when we had been out working. I was becoming more confident in myself about everything that I did, just being able to tell Sam to find the door and then to find the counter of a shop that was unknown to me. Sam did this with ease and going out of the shop again if anybody asked me if I needed help to find the door I was able to say with pride in Sam, " No thanks Sam will find the way ". We went to town about twice a week especially on market day to meet up with friends, do our shopping and return home on the bus. Sam became a regular visitor in the indoor market as we would stop at the same stalls not only to buy what I needed but because the staff were always wanting to chat about Sam and how I was getting on with him. People often told me that they either had a relative who did puppy walking or they sponsored a guide dog so I began to have to allow myself more time to go shopping because of all the people we met, very different to how it used to be when we went shopping before. We found more shops to go to that I had not been to for a long time so each day was different.

It was one day when we had gone into town and just past the bank which was always our first calling point. I told Sam that I wanted to go to a certain shop, it was the health food shop that we had visited many times before so Sam knew the way. As we walked along I guessed where I thought the shop was, as I could smell where the burger van was situated next to the shop and told Sam to find the door and he veered towards the right, stopped and sat down. I was puzzled as he had not done this before and I was sure that I was in the right place. Luckily I heard someone walking past and said " Can you tell me where the health food shop is? I think we are in the right place ". She chuckled as she said " Yes you are both in the right place, your dog is really good as the reason he has sat down is the shop has closed down and moved into the indoor centre next to the sports shop on the right next to the

My Journey To Freedom

café. If you can't find it I can come with you to help you ". We both laughed at this with Sam still sitting patiently waiting for the shop door to open! I told the woman thanks for helping but I could find my way. As we walked towards the shop I knew that Sam had shown me that, like on many more occasions that I was going to come across, I had to trust him completely in everything that he did and what he did was always for a reason. This time he had known where the shop was and not being able to find the door had done his best to tell me what I needed to know. I also realised that, because I was working with Sam and not struggling with a cane, I was able to think about this episode in a lighthearted manner. Kevin and I had a good laugh that evening and Sheila thought it was really funny.

I enjoyed spending time in the garden when the weather was favourable. Sam did not like it too hot as he had such a thick coat but as I wandered around doing jobs he was quite happy to be lying down where he could see me or to sit by my side which meant that he often got into my way when I was busy tending the borders. I began to feel his presence to be very companionable with Kevin away all day and the house was no longer so quiet as he followed me everywhere and I could always hear the sound of his paws following me. Before I had Sam I never went out for most of the day on a Monday, unless I could possibly help it, because it was rubbish day and the wheelie-bins were left all over the pavement so to try and negotiate them,

I either ended up with bruised legs or bumping into every one of them as I walked down the street. Sheila showed me how to go around the bins telling Sam to either find a way or to do an 'off-kerb manoeuvre', into the road and then back on to the pavement again after the obstacle had been passed. He really liked this as he had a lot to think about and very soon we were able to do this confidently and when Sam and I had been together for about a year, he could do this walk without me telling him what to do. I could sense and feel through the harness by his movement and pace of walking that he was judging what obstacles were ahead and then thinking about what he needed to do. Telling the instructor about this on my annual visit they said it was a sign of a good partnership together. So that was the end of being housebound on a Monday because of rubbish bins, another bit of freedom for me and it was marvellous having Sam.

Sam had his own way of avoiding people, mobility scooters and push chairs on the pavement. He would stop and sit down, waiting for them to go by and then carry on. Sheila told me this was all right as long as we were both safe. All guide dogs are trained in the same way but because they are also individuals they develop their own techniques when working. This is why it does take a long time to bond with your dog, eventually getting to know him like an extension of yourself when working. Sam was in his element when we went out as a family or by myself to a

My Journey To Freedom

crowded town centre, a busy car boot sale or fete. He quickened his pace immediately going through crowds so that sometimes I heard people having to sidestep suddenly to move out of his way. With his tail upright and moving confidently with me, people said that you could tell that he loved to work. How different to how it used to be for me. Sam did not mind other dogs when we were walking and would simply look in their direction and if I thought he was looking too much it only took a quick voice command from me and he would walk on. Sometimes when we passed another dog who was barking and straining on the lead to get to us causing its owner to get annoyed with it, Sam would have his tail erect and walk past the dog ignoring it completely as if to say to it "This is the way to behave!". If I was aware of someone with a dog coming towards me I would always be on my guard when the owners calmly said " Don't worry he's not on a lead, I've walked him for years along the pavement without one ". It only needed the dog to catch sight of a cat on the opposite side of the road to cause a road accident or for him to meet Sam and, taking an instant dislike to him, cause a fight. Sheila told me and I heard from other guide dog owners as well that sometimes when this situation occurred the guide dog had to be immediately retired as a result of the injuries sustained from the other dog or because the guide dog became too nervous to work. When this happened not only was it distressing to the owner, it forced a working dog to have to retire early and as a working guide dog costs about forty thousand pounds to look after throughout its life it was expensive as well as wasteful of the time and training spent on the dog.

    I did not mind when we met toddlers on bicycles riding on the pavement as they were usually with adults but it made Sam move suddenly if a child whizzed by us instead of cycling on the road. One day as we were walking along this happened and Sam suddenly stopped and nudged my leg as if he was telling me to move over, as the cyclist whizzed by shouting an apology. A passer by asked if we were all right and said that Sam had stopped me going forward because if I had sidestepped to avoid the cyclist I might have fallen over a couple of stones that had become dislodged from the low wall and fallen onto the pavement. I assured her that I was all right and we both grumbled about the wall, as it was well known that local teenagers liked to sit on it outside the shops so it had to be repaired quite frequently. I praised Sam and thought, not for the first time, that if I had used my cane I could have had a nasty fall or at least become disorientated by the experience as I walked along. Sheila had told me during training that Sam could be difficult because of his retriever breed but to be firm with him immediately and it shouldn't be a problem. I had finished sending Sheila monthly reports as six months had gone by already and Sheila said that we were settling down nicely, but I only had to phone her if I had a query

My Journey To Freedom

about Sam. We had already done a lot of short pavement walks to the shops so I became used to it, not so much that I took the walks and Sam's abilities for granted, but I knew that I was safe with Sam and could begin to listen more intently to my surroundings as a partnership together instead of feeling frustrated and having to concentrate so hard on where I was. It was wonderful to begin to enjoy simply going out for walks again, something that I had not felt for a very long time.

I spoke to Sam as we walked along telling him whereabouts we were going. He was always cautious and it took a long time to trust him every time that he stopped to tell me that something was blocking our path. It could be anything from a large twig, a dark patch of tarmac that contrasted to the normal colour because of workman resurfacing it, a pile of leaves or one day a pigeon in the town centre walking ahead of us and Sam stopped and waited until the bird had gone, which made several onlookers laugh. On another occasion he walking normally down the pavement when he began to veer from left to right and then right to left slowing his speed and being very cautious. I was just about to correct him as I could not hear or feel anything under my feet to account for his behaviour when a woman passing us said " Your dog is marvellous, I would have warned you but he has done such a good job. Someone must have dropped a bottle last night after coming out of the pub and there was broken glass scattered over the pavement and he guided you through it all ". I had not felt any glass at all where I had been walking and thanked the woman. Sam getting a well deserved fuss and a handful of his food pellets for a treat when he got home. I got Matthew, who was coming round for tea, to check his pads for any cuts but he was fine. There was one thing that I found annoying and throughout Sam's working life it happened from time to time, walking down the street to be confronted by a car owner or a workman outside a shop leaving their vehicle completely blocking the pavement so nobody could get past them. One day this happened several times walking down one stretch of road so each time I had to tell Sam to find a way by either turning back and crossing the road to avoid them or an " off kerb manoeuvre" . Sam managed without any problems but it was another occasion when I wondered how I would have coped with a cane. When I got home I still felt annoyed and got in touch with our local police support officer who sympathetically sorted the problem by having a word with the vehicle owners because it was not only myself who was effected but Mum's with push chairs or someone with a mobility scooter trying to get past that would have found it difficult.

Chapter 8
Adventures

Sam and I had been together for well over a year. Time was certainly rushing by us and my life had really changed for the better and the family and Kevin said that having Sam had really altered my life from what it had been like. It felt as if Sam and I had been partners for a longer period of time and I wished that perhaps I had thought of having a guide dog before so I could have avoided months of frustration. My heart condition was still causing problems but Kevin, knowing my love of gardening, suggested that for a holiday he would book a hotel near Maidenhead so that he could take me to visit Kew Gardens and other places around that area which I had been wanting to do for a long time but had never previously had the confidence or time to make the visit. He knew this area fairly well as he had grown up nearby so it was not a strange area for him but it was a new experience for us. I told Anne the instructor who visited us on our last annual visit about the trip and she said that Sam would enjoy it, as he liked new areas and experiences to discover. The annual visit was to solve any working problems that owners might have and to see how the owner and dog walked together by going for a short walk. This usually had to be done with some degree of deception because if the instructor came to the house first and then took the dog for a walk they knew what was going on and would be looking around to see where the instructor was, which created a false impression as to how they worked normally. So in most cases, Sam's included, whoever was coming for a visit would phone to say they had parked around the corner and I would tell them which route I was taking, so that they could observe from a distance without being spotted by the dog. This deception worked most of the time but as Sheila and Anne told me, nearly all the dogs seemed to know that someone from Guide Dogs had come so they were on their best behaviour.

The hotel near Maidenhead was nice and it was fortunate that we found a small pocket park five minutes walk away for Sam to use, so during our week away we spent time having lovely walks by the Thames, chatting to other dog owners as guide dogs were always an attraction or just sitting quietly with Sam and Kevin on the river bank as we listened to the swans who were regular visitors hoping for food scraps. We planned to spend the whole day at Kew Gardens and we were not

My Journey To Freedom

disappointed with warm weather and plenty of plants to feel and smell, buildings to look around and all the various garden designs to explore, having to stop for refreshments and to allow Sam to have a rest whenever we found a shady area for him. I remember that as we travelled back to our hotel base we were all tired but happy after a nice day out with Sam hardly moving for the rest of the evening. We went to see Windsor Castle and walking down the street we came across some street performers in fancy dress. Sam came to an abrupt halt looking very intently and staying very close to me until they had gone by. Around the next corner he came across a bagpipe player and reacted in the same way. It must have seemed very unusual to him but it showed how well the dogs are all trained in how they react to different situations. In the afternoon we took a small boat trip down the Thames to Windsor Races where we had a nice meal and Sam enjoyed people wanting to make a fuss of him when he wasn't working, watching everything going on around him including all the horse racing. That day was certainly one of Sam's most eventful of the week. The rest of the week we took a ride on a tour bus around the London sights and went to visit Brighton for the day, but I think Sam was glad to get back home to familiar surroundings, his own basket and toys!

We built up routines so that each day of the week I tried to go to different places so that Sam looked forward to working and did not have time to get bored. Going into town, visiting local markets, going shopping, visiting friends by bus for coffee or a meal then coming back home again, attending my blind social club meetings where Sam always had plenty of fuss. I always had to impress on people not to give him any biscuits if they asked me if they could give him one, explaining that it led to bad habits for them. Making friends with other guide dog owners who lived locally I was lucky that there was another person with their first guide dog so we were able to exchange tips and compare notes on how we were both progressing. Beginning to visit family who lived away from home, doing these journeys by train, I always had assistance as Sheila had advised so had no anxious feelings of whether I was on the right platform or catching the correct train when I had connections to make. Sam liked travelling by train and he was not too big to be able to curl up by my side out of people's way and go to sleep. He was always particularly careful stepping on to and out of the train doorway as some trains had a deep step or there was a drop if the platform was low. He would put his front legs up on to the doorway step and stop, which told me how deep the step was, and then carry on when he knew that I had stepped up by his side. He did this getting on and off buses, which was really useful to me when the driver could not park near the kerb, and out of the trains, unless I had been told that there was a longer drop than normal and then I held his lead and he had to step out of the

My Journey To Freedom

train and wait for me to join him, though there was always a guard or other passengers to help if I needed it.

When Sam and I went to meetings or to church he was always well behaved, lying down with his eyes half closed but attentive, though he did have a habit of wagging his tail with quick movements when he thought we had been there for long enough. It did not cause any disruption except that it sounded like a dull thump if the room had wooden flooring, but people sitting nearby would say to me afterwards that they did not need a watch to tell them it was nearing the end of the meeting, they just had to listen for Sam!

Sam loved his free run times in the park. I had a choice of taking him to the small pocket park ten minutes away from home, the dog run attached to the park in Market Harborough, only a bus ride away which I combined with a shopping trip as well if I had time between buses, or a large park on the outskirts of Kettering. If it was a nice day and I wanted a walk with no shopping to do we went up several side streets past some grass areas that were around and returning through an alleyway by the parish church in town. I knew that this alleyway had yew trees and overgrown shrubs commonly found in parts of old churchyards and if you were quiet you could hear squirrels scampering in and dashing up and down the trees or running quickly across the path. Sam walked along and suddenly would look intently towards where obviously he could see them, never growling or barking, but I often wondered if he thought they might be fun to play with. Every time we walked along that alleyway he eagerly looked around expecting to see them. Crossing the road was now a lot easier, apart from having to concentrate on days when the wind was blowing and it was raining as this made it difficult to listen for any traffic coming, or to cope with road works or delivery lorries parked in the wrong place. Sam refused to cross the road at our normal crossing point to go to the local market one day. I told Sam to go forward several times but he would not move, so I waited until I heard a person going past and asked them if they could see anything that I could not hear. After a pause he said, " Well the only thing I can see is a large plastic bag blowing down the road ". We waited until he said the road was clear and I told Sam again to go forward and, this time, he did. I sometimes think that he can be too cautious but that is better than him taking any risks if he is not sure of something.

One of the things I had to get used to was when I first qualified and Sheila was showing us different routes, or we went to a town shopping with friends, was finding public toilets. Sam not only had to find the right one as male and female ones usually were situated next door to each other and the symbols on the door were not tactile enough to distinguish between them, but sometimes it was a tight squeeze to fit Sam and myself into the cubicle space. Occasionally I had to resort to making Sam sit outside the cubicle door and slipping his lead under the door to hold on to if there was no one to hold him. Having a guide dog always started conversations and one day a woman in the toilets at the same time asked me, " How does the dog know the difference between the male and female toilets, has he ever got it wrong ?" I replied after a little thought with a smile " He hasn't got it wrong yet ". We both laughed and went our separate ways. Life had certainly become more amusing with a dog. I solved these problems by obtaining a Radar Key from the council that I could use for the larger disabled toilets that were usually nearby.

Where I live I am lucky that there are some footpaths and bridle ways I can use to give Sam a change from walking on pavements and often we would be walking along and disturb rabbits crossing our path or pass someone on horseback. Over two or three months we met the same rider on the same bridle way quite regularly and Sam, not being alarmed by a big horse would stop and sit down, waiting for the horse to go by wagging his tail slightly as if he was pleased to see a new friend. Meeting other dog owners did not cause any problems and they would often want to stop and chat or make a compliment about how well Sam was doing. Even with his stubborn moments he had an easy-going character and was able to cope with any difficult situations we had encountered so far.

CHAPTER 9

Facing Difficulties

For some time my heart condition had been causing more problems so I was finding that I could not take Sam for long walks as I had been doing and was having to be careful in how much I did each day. Sam did not mind a change in routine some days and was content to just be with me. We had to cancel any plans for a holiday in 2003 and we had some day trips out by coach to the seaside instead. Sam enjoyed these, as he always worked well in different locations and we did not want to walk very far, but when it came to a leisurely stroll on the pier he became very hesitant as he started to walk on the wooden planking and we realised it was because he could see the waves below through the narrow gaps in between the planks as well as hearing the noise it made. It took a little gentle persuasion with some food treats and coaxing to get on to the pier with him. When we walked back in the same direction

My Journey To Freedom

later in the day to catch the coach home he had no problem walking on to the pier again.

I had been advised to have a pacemaker fitted, as medication was not successful, so in the summer of 2004 I had it fitted. I knew that I would not be able to work with Sam for about six weeks as I had to let it heal up and as it was inserted by my left collarbone and I worked Sam on my left I knew that I had to be patient with myself. Easier said than done, as going back to using a cane would be like going back to the beginning without Sam even if it was only going to be for a short while. I arranged with Matthew and Kevin to take Sam for walks when they could and Kevin took him for longer walks at the weekend. Sam could walk on the lead but became easily distracted by smells and kept looking around for me and wondering, I expect, why he wasn't working on harness with me. I had to be content with giving him plenty of fuss with some obedience training each day. I phoned Anne at Guide Dogs because I was anxious about Sam working again after a long break and asked her if he might need retraining. I remember she said quite confidently " Have more faith in Sam. He is such a good worker, I can't see there will be any problems. It will be best for the first few walks to be short so that he gets used to the harness again ". I felt relieved by what she had said, but of course she was experienced in dealing with different situations and had probably come across this problem with dogs many times before. I would just have to wait and see what happened.

It was frustrating going back to my old mode of mobility. My anxieties and concerns began to creep back again, together with a much slower pace of walking that I found annoying. Even though I knew it would not be for very long, I immediately realised just how much Sam had changed my life, not only by being my constant companion when Kevin was at work but in the way he gave me my independence back each day and the freedom he gave me through not having to rely on other people so much. I began to think that it must be very difficult emotionally for guide dog owners who through health problems or ill health of the dog had to stop working suddenly and perhaps never be able to have a working dog again. It would be very depressing and I hoped that I would never have to face that particular problem.

After having the all-clear from the doctors that I could work with Sam again, I decided after talking it over with Kevin that I would start to take Sam as far as the post box and back again, to see how he was back in harness and would walk him in the evening time when it was getting dark, to make Sam concentrate more on where he was going. I did feel a bit apprehensive when I put Sam's harness on him for the first time and we started to work together again. A little way down the street he shook himself as if to say holiday time is over and it's back to working again. His tail went up and he started walking, quickly obedient at each

My Journey To Freedom

command I gave him. On the second evening he was eager to have his harness back on and raring to go for our walk. I need not have worried after all about him and he proved that my worries about his working capabilities were groundless. People often asked me what Sam was like when he was not working and off harness at home. I told them that he was like any normal family dog playing with his toys, dashing around playing and wanting a fuss, but as soon as he knew I was going out or I went to get his harness and lead from behind the door it was instantaneous, the change in his behaviour from playing to working, eager to have his harness on and wanting to know where we were going to. We started to build up our routines again but while I was wary about how I was coping with the pacemaker, Sam was pleased to be working once more and his tail was constantly wagging as we walked along.

We went on several coach trips organised by different clubs that I or Kevin belonged to, mainly to various garden centres and to the seaside. On one trip, when we had stopped at a garden centre for a refreshment break on the way to the seaside for the weekend, we all had to get off the coach at one end of the car park that was not an authorized dropping off point because of the volume of traffic that had built up. The driver told us that he had to find a suitable parking place for the coach and, at the time we had arranged to meet up again, would try and find a place near to where he had dropped us off, if possible. After our break we all walked to the entrance and other people started to look for the coach. There were several coaches the same as the one we had come in and a lot of traffic and several people were saying in such a crowded place it was going to be difficult to find the right coach. I knew that Sam had the ability of being able to find cars that we had travelled in before so I told Sam to " Find the coach! ". He looked around, getting his bearings and headed off the way we had come in to the car park, moving through the traffic and then starting to go in a different direction and after a few minutes we had arrived at the coach. I was pleased that Sam had managed to do it and gave him a fuss. The driver was surprised to see us and said that he had not been able to come to tell us where he was because of leaving the coach, in case he had to move it quickly because of the traffic. Unknown to me until we had arrived at the coach, several people had noticed Sam trying to find the coach and had decided to follow us, so it was a bit like the Pied Piper with everybody following behind. The incident of " Sam being able to find the coach" became a talking point for several months when we met up with friends that we had not seen for a while and reminisced about our coach trips and what we had been doing.

I became a grandmother when Caron had a little boy just after Christmas, another addition to the family and more visits to make when they were both settled back home again.

My Journey To Freedom

It was about this time, when I had been to a garden club meeting, that I met Julie who was also interested in gardening and she was the secretary of the local Guide Dog fundraising branch. After introducing herself and asking all about Sam she inquired if I would be interested in becoming involved with the branch as they did a lot of fundraising by street collecting, outside supermarkets, stalls at fetes and the indoor shopping centre near Christmas time. Some of the members also talked to schools, clubs and youth organisations like Brownies, Beavers and Cubs, to raise awareness of the work that guide dogs do. Offer help with any fundraising events that they would be interested in doing and collecting any donations the clubs or schools had collected as a result of helping Guide Dogs. I told Julie that I would be interested in becoming involved and would like to help out at the next street collection.

I enjoyed our first collection. Sam had an extra brush making sure that he looked smart and he behaved himself by lying quietly and pleased to have some unexpected fuss made of him. It was common practice to pair someone with a dog with another person so that there was someone to chat to, hand out stickers and hold another collecting tin if there were a lot of people during the two hour stints. The collection was the start of Sam and I becoming involved with the branch, widening our horizons even more and making many friends.

CHAPTER 10
Changes

Sam and I took part in several collections mainly outside different supermarkets as the street collections were only held once or twice a year. I got used to people asking lots of questions concerning Sam, about the length of his training, about Guide Dogs in general and it was nice to meet different members of the public and make them more aware of Guide Dogs and the work that they do. We started to go to primary schools to listen to others in the group talk to the children during assemblies. Usually it involved giving them a brief outline of what a Guide Dog was for and how they worked and then question and answer time with the children who had questions already prepared with the help of the teachers. Sometimes after the assembly we took the dogs around some of the classrooms to meet more of the children and we handed out a few posters of Guide Dogs for them to put up on the wall. If we went to Brownies or Cubs it was similar talks about Guide Dogs as they were usually working for different badges to do with either community or disabilities. Depending on the age of the children we handed out Guide Dog badges as well. It was not until I had become involved with Guide Dogs that I realised after meeting and making friends with various guide dog puppy-walkers how much work they put into bringing up a puppy until it was ready if accepted for its advanced training to become a guide dog. I knew a little about puppy walkers before but not the amount of work they do, first of all having to carry their puppies around until they have their inoculations, getting them used to wearing a collar and lead, teaching them basic commands like left and right. One of the most time consuming but important parts of the basic training, to learn 'busy-busy', which is the command that all guide dogs learn, to spend before and when they return from a walk so that they do not have accidents when they are walking and then, of course, when they are with their new owners and are working. They have to socialize the puppies, taking them into shops, doctors, dentists, lifts, getting them used to different noises like fireworks, cars backfiring, general noise and bustle in a town centre, journeys by car and train as well as putting up with the destructive tendencies that all puppies have. Then, when they have grown to love their puppy, trained and looked after it for about a year, they have to give it back to the instructors at Guide Dogs for its advanced training.

If they are prepared to have another puppy they are normally given one as soon as they return the previous one to Guide Dogs and so the process starts again. Since Guide Dogs is self-funded and does not receive any government funding the cost of the training each puppy is about five thousand pounds.

Julie's husband Bill who is chairman of the branch asked several of us if we would like to go on a speaker's course for Guide Dogs. More people were making enquiries for speakers at schools and clubs and the branch, being made up of volunteers, had not enough speakers to go round. Sam had given me so much more confidence that after listening to the others talking in schools I said that I would like to attend the course. So in March 2005, we all travelled by car to Edmondscote Manor where I had qualified with Sam. The course was held over two days, which meant quite a bit of travelling and involved us giving two separate talks, listening to the others talking and getting feedback, advice and tips on how to present talks. Sam had a nice time as when we had refreshment breaks Sam was taken for a walk with another guide dog by a member of staff. We all passed the course and had to have criminal record and police checks to make sure that we were suitable to be with children. The first couple of times that I helped to give a talk to children I felt nervous and then as comes with practice we settled down into a routine of Bill giving a small talk on Guide Dogs, altering it depending

My Journey To Freedom

on the age of the audience, then one of the puppy walkers would talk about training a puppy and I talked about what it was like to be a Guide Dog owner and what Sam got up to, emphasising how important Sam was to me giving me my freedom and independence and how I had to trust him over one hundred percent with my life. Each branch had their own way of giving talks but we found that this way gave a broader outlook to the audience instead of only one person talking. While I talked Sam was quietly lying on the floor usually with his eyes open watching what was going on. Sometimes I demonstrated to the children how I held the handle of the harness so I could feel what Sam was doing and to guide him as well. If there was time when we visited a school and with the teacher's permission the children were allowed to come up to the dogs in a line and stroke them if they wanted to. Sam of course was eager afterwards to find Bill's car for his ride home.

I had been having regular appointments at the hospital but after having to have a couple of emergency hospital admissions it was decided that the pacemaker could not fully correct the problem so a few months after the speakers course I had an ablation procedure done on the heart and it meant another period of not being able to work with Sam until I had begun to feel better again. I stopped being involved with the Guide Dog branch for a few weeks, which I missed, until I felt better but I knew that it was better for me if I did not overdo things. When I was able to work with Sam again

I noticed that he seemed to be getting tired after his walks and he started to have a few stomach upsets as well. At nearly six years of age at this time, I thought it might be his age but took him to see his old friend John who still worked at the vets. A few months previously the vets had opened another branch in the town where I lived so it was convenient for me just being able to walk him to the vets instead of having to catch a bus, see the vet and then wait for the bus to come home again. After having blood tests and x-rays, John said that he had some irritable bowel/liver problems that the larger breeds of dog can sometimes get and this was causing him to lose weight as he couldn't absorb nutrients properly. His diet was changed and extra supplements were given but it took a long time before John was pleased with the way he was progressing and his tests were normal. As a working dog owner, just handling the dog each day or holding the harness and feeling how he was working could tell you usually if something was wrong with the dog, but as the dog advisor from Guide Dogs who help with any problems or give advice after you had qualified said, some dogs worked even when they were quite ill because that was their job and they would not give in. Sam did not have to give up working but I altered our routine so that he had shorter walks to do. We carried on with collections and school talks and we all became more proficient as we gained experience with each talk that we gave, in judging the length of each talk, what to say depending on the age of the children and how much time we were allocated in the assemblies.

It had now been nearly three years since Kevin and I had had a break and we both felt that we needed a holiday. My health problems had improved enough so that we both felt it was all right to travel farther afield than we had been doing and I felt that I was getting weary with the same routines. Kevin planned a surprise weekend away after Christmas, when we had a few bright days in the early part of January to see how I coped with travelling and doing extra walking and we went away to a small old fashioned town called Oakham in Rutland, near enough to come home if I had any problems. It was a town with historical buildings and a market place with the atmosphere that the town had developed over the years but it had not lost its old world charm. Sam enjoyed exploring a different area going along alleyways and visiting the local museum and church. I don't think that he was very keen on some areas of the market place as the cobbled stones were awkward for him to walk on but he was so eager to explore around that it did not cause any problems. The hotel owner made us feel welcome, making a fuss of Sam and we both returned home feeling much better after our break.

Chapter 11
People And Places

Sam continued to improve and we were busy doing a lot of talks at schools. He made us laugh as Bill always went in first to say that we had arrived and to sign in, then the teacher would either take us to the assembly hall or if we were a little early have a coffee in the staff room. Sam always tried to walk ahead to be first into the hall even when he did not know the way and coming out of schools he would frequently suddenly stop so I would have to ask the others why. It varied between a painted line across the pathway marking out part of the playground, a dark patch of tarmac, leaves and twigs and later that year during the autumn, we went to a large school that had a long driveway surrounded by parkland and trees. As we walked along the driveway Sam came to an abrupt halt and seemed to be looking at me. I asked the others why he had stopped and they said the driveway was covered with conkers that had fallen from the trees that lined the drive and they were scattered all over the place. Someone said perhaps he was looking at me for guidance as he knew that he could not guide me through all the conkers. Just then some pupils approached and they said they had come to meet us to take us to the right room, so we asked them if they could kick some of the conkers away and make a path. I told Sam to go forward and he went carefully weaving in and out of the conkers and I did not feel any underfoot as I went along. This incident became another talking point at school and club talks, as a way to tell our audience how cautious guide dogs could be when they were guiding someone. Quite often after talks at W.I. or other club meetings people would come up to us and say how much they had enjoyed the talk and how could they help to fund raise, become a puppy walker or how to sponsor a puppy. I was always pleased about this and hoped just by talking to the general public I could perhaps encourage another visually impaired person to make inquiries about a guide dog and be able to experience the freedom and independence that Sam had given to me. Often I would be in one of the nearby towns shopping with Sam and pass a group of children or children with their families and hear them say, " There is the lady with Sam who gave us a talk at school " or we would be standing in a shop queue somewhere and a child with her family would come up to us and say, " Hello, can I stroke Sam? You talked at Brownies the other evening ". I always said that, as long as

Sam was not working, he was just standing in a queue and I was not holding the harness handle, they could give Sam a fuss.

After going away to Oakham Kevin suggested that I went on one of the Garden weekends organised by Thrive -- The National Blind Gardeners' Club. I had been a member for several years and always had their quarterly audio magazine and often phoned them for tips and advice that I needed. I knew that they organised weekend and day garden courses which were partly funded by the lottery fund and that these were held all over the country and staffed by Thrive and volunteers. I had never before attending one due to a lot of reasons of finance, not having the confidence to travel and go to a strange place using a cane and my health in recent years. So Sam and I went on our travels again leaving Kevin to look after himself, which he did not mind. We went by train and were met by staff at Nottingham as the course was held at the University. I was shown around the centre by one of the volunteers and told there was a special area set aside for the dogs for spending. It did not matter that I did not know anybody as everybody was very friendly with a number of other guide dog owners there so it was possible to let some of the dogs have a free run together. The course lasted all day Saturday followed by a garden quiz and on Sunday we had a short course followed by garden question and answers relevant to gardening for blind gardeners. Then we all travelled home by

My Journey To Freedom

various means, some of us struggling with plants and garden items we had made.

It was a busy year with visiting family by train as well as having visitors. Caron came round quite often and Sam enjoyed playing with Joshua even though I was careful because Sam was a lot bigger than him. We decided to go to Jersey on holiday as well. We knew the area fairly well as we had been there several years ago and now that my health had improved and I had Sam it would be a nice holiday. I had advice from Guide Dogs and the vets and I did not need a pet passport for Sam. We had to book flights, as this was easier for us than going by ferry and also tell the airline that we had a guide dog. You would have thought that Sam had been a frequent traveller by air as he was quite content to lie down by my side as we waited for our flight to be called and he did not mind the noise, hustle and bustle of a busy airport. He followed the member of staff who showed us the way to the plane steps confidently and walked into the cabin settling down where a spare seat had been reserved for us to give him more room to lie down and after the plane took off he went to sleep. A number of passengers did not realise that he was on board and the cabin staff said they wished all the passengers were as quiet as Sam. We all had a good holiday with the hotel staff Philip and Christina making us all feel very welcome and, after exploring places that we had visited before, Sam had got used to the area and could find his way back to the hotel and the bus station without any problems. We went on a couple of coach trips, as we had not got a car and it was a good idea to see as much as possible of the island. A few days later we were walking in the town centre and a couple said, " Hello, there is Sam who was on our coach trip " . People remembered Sam even if they forgot our names. One of the places we visited was the German Underground Hospital, which the Germans had built during the Second World War using prisoners of war. The inside was very dark which did not bother me but people were getting lost and in some of the rooms they had air raid sirens and noises of bombs going off. Sam did not get confused or mind the noise and took it all in his stride. Since that visit they have changed the inside of the hospital as we have been back recently with Sam.

Sam loved going on the beach playing with other dogs who were there but typical Sam he did not like the sea and if I went in for a paddle he kept out of the waves but as close to me on the sand, as he could. We often went by the Victorian market place and after passing it a couple of times Sam suddenly stopped outside a small shop that was next door and refused to move. I asked Kevin what he thought the matter was and he burst out laughing, " I think Sam is trying to tell you something, after a busy day out he has stopped outside the pet shop for a treat " so I had to go in and get him a small treat. Sam certainly was a character. We have been to Jersey again

My Journey To Freedom

since that visit and he always made a bee-line for that shop if we were near the market. St. Helier, the central town in Jersey, had a few small market squares and we were passing through one of them on the way back to the hotel one afternoon when Sam suddenly stopped moving closer to my legs. I asked Kevin what he thought Sam had seen, as Sam seemed to be looking at something. Kevin said, " The only thing I can think of is that there are two full size concrete cows in the middle of the square. Perhaps he thinks they should be in a field ". I told Sam it was all right and we walked along the side of the market square slowly past the cows and then turned around and back the same way and he seemed more at ease. I took him back on purpose the next day to see what his reaction would be and he was fine and not bothered at all. We both said that Sam had an eventful holiday.

I told Anne all about it during her annual visit and how pleased I was that Sam had been so at ease with flying and Anne said of course it is not part of their training to go on planes normally, unless Guide Dogs are taking dogs over to the Channel Isles for their new owners, but because their character is easy-going and with all their social training they cope with most situations, but that is why it does take two years to train them.

Chapter 11

A Dignified Ending

Time had gone by and it was hard to believe that I had Sam for six years. Anne said on her last visit that when they get to around eight years old, which Sam was approaching, they do start to look more closely at how they work so they can tell if they are tiring easily because they are getting older and have to retire. It was something that I did not want to start to think about just yet and I hoped that I would have Sam for a long time, as the dogs did not generally retire until they were nearing ten and sometimes eleven years of age. When I thought of everything I had accomplished since I had Sam and looked back at how I had felt and what I was doing with my life before, it was easy to see how Sam had walked into my life and transformed it for the better.

A lot of people had been asking for Guide Dogs' speakers so Bill was busy making arrangements to visit more schools and clubs. We visited a lot of schools that we had been to the previous year as they had taken part in events or raised money for Guide Dogs by different sponsored events and they had got donations that they wanted to give to us. Many of the children remembered the dogs if they had not moved to different schools, Sam still liked all the attention and of course everybody wanted to know all about the puppies. For the last couple of years Bill and Julie had a stall at our local carnival and I told Bill if he was busy getting things ready for the afternoon I would walk down to the recreation ground and meet them there so I could support them. I could not help behind the stall but everybody wanted to know about Sam and ask generally about Guide Dogs so it did tend to draw people in to buy items at the stall. As usual it was crowded going down to the carnival with people lining the streets waiting for the floats to go by and we arrived at the entrance to the park and of course I did not know where Bill had put up the stall so I told Sam, " Find Bill's car ". He immediately picked up his speed and went off in a certain direction, and very soon he could hear one of the puppies barking as one of the puppy walkers was there and Sam arrived in front of the stall and Bill's car. Bill and everybody were surprised at Sam but as Bill had said in the past he was always amazed at what a Guide Dog could do.

I went on another Thrive garden weekend to Wiltshire, meeting old friends and making new ones as well, the course was run on the same lines as before so I had a busy but very enjoyable time.

Kevin and I decided that we could manage to have two trips away so we went to Jersey in the spring again because I wanted to go around the Lavender Farm enjoying the wonderful smells of the lavender and rosemary bushes. Visiting other gardens with all the spring flowers and garden designs and the colourful gardens along the pier front at Gorey Harbour that were full of spring bedding plants. We went back to other places we had visited before and had nice walks along the coastal paths that we had not discovered on previous holidays. This time Sam did not meet any concrete cows but he found the pet shop again and for the first time he had a ride in a steam train at an exhibition. I'm not sure that he was very keen on the ride as it rattled a lot as it bumped along. On the flight back home the cabin crew were at the entrance to the plane and made a big fuss of Sam as he found the correct seats that they said were ours.

During the summer I travelled to Birmingham for the weekend to see Matthew who had moved near there with his fiance Mary and we had a busy pleasant weekend, taking us to visit other family members, a craft exhibition and a garden centre. We travelled by train to see other friends and to go on shopping trips with them to other cities. During the summer I started a college course one morning a week to learn how to use a computer with a screen reader as I felt that I was getting

My Journey To Freedom

left behind by modern technology, not entirely my own fault as any sort of equipment or modern gadget that is adapted for visually impaired people is always very expensive. Sam of course had to learn the new route to the college and during my lesson he curled up contentedly under the desk. When we finished our course each week I would take Sam for a run in the park or meet a friend in town.

One day we went to the vets in town for Sam's usual check-up and as I opened the door the receptionist said urgently, " Don't come in, I've just spilt water on the floor and I'm clearing it up "

Before I had the chance to give Sam a command of what I wanted him to do he swung his body round in front of my legs so that I could not move forward and stayed in that position keeping me out of danger. The receptionist asked me if we were all right and I replied that we were. The receptionist said that the floor was still wet and as Sam had not moved I said that we would make another appointment for another day. I praised Sam telling him to turn around and we would go home. Kevin said that he knew that Sam would always protect and keep me safe and that incident proved it. A lot of building work had been going on in the town with new houses and flats springing up everywhere. This of course from time to time caused a lot of disruption to pedestrians so I could walk down a street one day and it would be perfectly clear and the following day the road or the pavement would be dug up with signs and traffic lights causing the traffic to either build up or having to find another way and cause traffic chaos in another part of town. It happened one day when I had been visiting a friend and the pavement was blocked in places with scaffolding put up ready for more building work. I had been told about this by my friend as we were leaving so as we were walking along and I could hear more noise I told Sam to find a way. He carefully walked along, weaving in and out of the obstacles, not paying any attention to all the noise of diggers and lorries and before I knew it we had walked alongside the scaffolding and a workman's voice said, " I was just going to ask if you needed any help along here. Your dog's great, the way he works, so I can see that you're ok". Sam carried on as if he had done this every day, walking along busy and difficult road works.

In September we went back to Jersey again for the second time, as we wanted to meet up with some friends and visit the Jersey Air Show that we had never seen before. We hoped to find an area away from the main airport but close enough to the beach to be able to enjoy what was going on and not too noisy for Sam. There were plenty of pathways and side streets we could take to get away from the beach area if the planes became to loud. We had one day-trip and caught the ferry to Guernsey. We had comfortable seats and were not troubled by sea sickness at all, including Sam of course who lay down on the floor relaxed and looking all around him at most other people who

My Journey To Freedom

were rushing upstairs to the top deck to get some fresh air. We had a nice couple of hours exploring round, taking a coach trip as it was the quickest way to get the feel of the island. We went on a trip to see the gardens at Sameres Manor, an old Manor House with craft exhibitions and beautiful Japanese, Water-Rock, Exotic, and Herb gardens as well as a cafe that sold lovely home made food. Even Kevin who is not a gardener but likes our garden to look nice enjoyed looking around. The highlight of the day for me was we had stopped for lunch and a break for Sam and we heard some people mention there was a guided tour around the herb garden during the afternoon. I went along to the meeting point at the scheduled time as Kevin wanted to look at other things and no one else turned up so Sam and I had a personal one-to-one guided tour by one of the head gardeners which I thoroughly enjoyed.

Back home we had several school talks to do and I was asked to go to the World Conker Championships which is held in Northamptonshire in the small village of Ashton. The Guide Dog branch had a stall there among other charity stalls. It was really crowded as it was held on the village green with a lot of people dressed up for the event and displays of Morris dancing. In another area near the church an instructor from Guide Dogs had obstacles in a display enclosure and blindfolded members of the public so that they could walk with a guide dog with a harness on to see what it was like. This attracted a lot of older children and adults so there was always a long queue for this attraction.

The months passed quickly as they often do around Christmas, when there is so much to do. Sam had his annual visit and I said he seemed to be getting a little tired but that was fairly normal as he was now getting older and Anne said she might start to monitor him more closely. January and February were the usual winter times of taking Sam for a walk, avoiding the early morning hard frosts that were slippery underfoot and getting fed up stuck indoors whenever we had the snow and frozen snow making the pavements very icy. We had two twisting corners in our side street before we could get onto the main road leading down the hill into town. Because of this the sun would only melt certain patches on the pavement, so even when we had only a medium covering of snow it took a long time for the pavements to thaw out, especially with children sliding and having fun on the way to school, so people were walking in the road when the paths were really bad. I took the sensible approach and did not venture out with Sam when the pavements were icy or a friend would phone and say that people were falling over in the centre of town because of the conditions. Kevin kept me informed as well and would phone me from work about the weather unless it was too bad for me to go out. It just wasn't worth the risk going out and falling over so Sam and I would stay indoors waiting rather impatiently for better weather.

My Journey To Freedom

It was quite by chance one day when I had brushed Sam and was putting his collar on that I thought I felt a lump well hidden by his thick retriever coat on the front of his neck. I took him down to see John who examined his neck and thought he felt it as well. He said come back in a month and we will see if it has grown. I walked home with Sam with a sinking feeling in my stomach and hoped that it would turn out to be a harmless cyst and not a tumour. I rang Kevin at work and told him. The family were concerned and my friends at the Guide Dog branch were supportive and hoped that he would be all right. I informed the Guide Dog advisor who deals with any problems the dogs might have and we all hoped for the best. The month appeared to go by slowly and Sam seemed fine working as John said that it would be all right for him to continue. John's voice sounded concerned when he next examined him saying the lump had grown a lot in the month, which was not a good sign and it really needed to be removed as soon as possible. A couple of days later he operated and said he had to send it away to the laboratory for examination but he was sure that it had been malignant and was on the thyroid gland in the neck. Sam came home on the same day after his operation unsure on his feet but wagging his tail. We were all upset and trying not to show it in front of Sam as he would sit tightly against me with his nose on my lap if he thought that I was unhappy. A couple of months went by and there was no sign of any

Maura Walsh

recurring tumours but when Anne came to see us I said that Sam still wanted to work. John said it was all right to do short walks but he had slowed down and seemed to tire easily.

After a lot of thinking between Anne and the Guide Dog advisor, a lot of soul searching and the family being upset as well, thinking about the right thing to do, we decided that Sam should retire and be re-homed with one of the foster families that Guide Dogs have a waiting list for dogs to go to. I did have a choice of either keeping Sam and go on the waiting list for another dog or to decide to have him re-homed. As Anne and I talked about it, it was not very practical for me to keep Sam when Kevin was out at work all day and he would be left on his own a lot when I was working with a new dog. Also if the dog had been a good worker they can feel depressed when they have always worked and then another dog comes along and takes over their role. Some owners do keep their dogs when they have retired but they always have partners or family at home during the day making this easier. Sometimes if suitable a member of the family take on the dog when they retire if they live nearby.

So it was in May of 2008 that Sam left to begin what I hope will be a long and happy retirement. It was a very difficult decision for me to make, knowing that it was the most sensible practical solution to the problem, but I had had Sam for nearly seven years of his life and we had not only faced many adventures and challenges together

My Journey To Freedom

but we had bonded and he seemed a part of me when we were working together. I could almost tell what he was thinking and he seemed to know what I wanted from him. In return though he had given me my freedom, independence and had been a loyal companion. I had been able to find an inner confidence to achieve so much more than I am certain I would have done without him. I am sure that I will always remember him, even when I have another Guide Dog and we become partners with a strong bond together. I *will* always look back *on Sam my first dog* as the one who took me on my journey to freedom.

Epilogue

Sam has settled down happily in his retirement home.

I now have another Guide Dog, but that may be a different story.

Acknowledgement

The author would like to thank her family and friends for all their support and encouragement when writing. Kevin for his advice and Bill and Julie for their words of wisdom.